Mastering
GIMP 3

The Ultimate Beginners and Seniors Guide to
Image Editing and Graphic Design

Tova Greg

Table of Contents

Chapter 1

Getting Started with GIMP 3

What is GIMP?

GIMP, which stands for **GNU Image Manipulation Program**, is a free and open-source graphics editor used for tasks such as photo retouching, image composition, and image authoring. Whether you're a hobbyist photographer, a digital artist, a graphic designer, or someone looking to create compelling social media content, GIMP offers powerful tools to help you achieve professional-quality results without the hefty price tag of commercial software like Adobe Photoshop.

Originally developed in 1995 by two university students, GIMP has grown into a full-featured image editing platform supported by a vast community of developers and artists. Its open-source nature means it's continuously being improved, and its capabilities can be extended with plug-ins, scripts, and custom tools. With the release of **GIMP 3**, users are welcomed with an even more refined and modernized interface, improved performance, and expanded features that cater to both beginners and professionals.

Key Features and Capabilities

GIMP 3 comes loaded with a variety of features that make it a standout choice among image editors:

1. Comprehensive Editing Tools GIMP provides a rich set of editing tools, including brushes, pencils, airbrushes, cloning, and a wide selection of selection tools (lasso, rectangular, elliptical, fuzzy select, etc.). These tools allow you to edit images with precision and control.

2. Layer-Based Editing Layers are the building blocks of non-destructive editing. You can add multiple images or design elements to different layers, adjust their opacity, blend modes, and use layer masks for advanced compositions.

3. High-Quality Photo Manipulation From retouching skin and removing blemishes to changing backgrounds and altering colors, GIMP allows for complex photo manipulation. Tools like the Healing Brush, Clone Tool, and

Perspective Tool are ideal for perfecting photographs.

4.   Advanced   Color   Management
GIMP supports high-fidelity color reproduction through full support for color profiles. This ensures your images maintain accurate colors on different devices and platforms.

5.   Custom   Brushes   and   Patterns
You can use built-in brushes or create your own. The same applies to patterns and gradients, giving you endless creative freedom when painting or filling spaces in your design.

6.   Plug-ins   and   Extensibility
GIMP's functionality can be extended with a wide range of plug-ins and scripts. Whether you're looking to automate tasks, add filters, or incorporate third-party features, GIMP is highly customizable.

7.   Cross-Platform   and   Lightweight
GIMP runs smoothly on Windows, macOS, and Linux systems. It's lightweight compared to many commercial editors, making it a great option for systems with limited resources.

8.   Format   Support
GIMP supports many file formats, including

JPEG, PNG, GIF, TIFF, PSD (Photoshop), and even raw image formats via plug-ins. It also has its own native format, XCF, which preserves layers and other editable elements.

With these tools at your disposal, GIMP 3 is ready to handle everything from simple photo corrections to complex digital artwork.

Downloading and Installing GIMP 3

Getting GIMP 3 up and running on your system is straightforward. Here's a step-by-step guide for downloading and installing the software:

Step 1: Visit the Official Website Go to the official GIMP website: This is the safest and most reliable source to download the latest version of the software.

Step 2: Choose Your Operating System Click on the "Download" button. The website will automatically detect your operating system (Windows, macOS, or Linux) and provide the appropriate installer. If not, you can manually choose your platform from the options provided.

Step 3: Start the Download Click the download link to begin the file transfer. Depending on your internet speed, this may take a few moments as the installer file is several hundred megabytes in size.

Step 4: Run the Installer
Once the download is complete, open the installer file. Follow the on-screen instructions to proceed with the installation. You can choose standard or custom options based on your preferences, such as the installation path or language.

Step 5: Launch GIMP
After installation, launch the program. The first time GIMP runs, it may take a few seconds longer to load as it initializes fonts and system resources.

Overview of the User Interface

When you open GIMP 3 for the first time, you'll notice that its user interface has evolved significantly from previous versions. It's cleaner, more intuitive, and offers a single-window mode by default — a welcome improvement for new users who may have been overwhelmed by GIMP's older multi-window layout.

1. Toolbox (Left Panel)
This is where most of the tools are located — Move, Crop, Text, Brush, Eraser, and more. Each

tool is represented by an icon, and hovering over it gives you a tooltip. When you select a tool, its options appear below the toolbox or in a separate area, giving you control over how the tool behaves.

2.   Canvas   (Center)
This is the main workspace where you view and edit your images. When you open or create a file, it appears here. You can zoom in and out, rotate, and pan around your image as needed.

3.   Tool   Options   (Below   Toolbox)
Every tool has its own customizable settings. For example, when using the brush tool, you can change the size, hardness, and dynamics here. This panel gives fine control over each tool's behavior.

4. Layers, Channels, Paths, and Undo (Right Panel)
This section helps you manage your layers and other important image components.

- **Layers Tab**: Shows a stack of your image's layers.
- **Channels Tab**: Displays color channels (Red, Green, Blue).
- **Paths Tab**: For vector paths created with the Path tool.

- **Undo History Tab**: Lets you undo or redo multiple steps quickly.

5.   Menu   Bar   (Top)
The menu bar gives access to all the features GIMP has to offer. Categories include File, Edit, Select, View, Image, Layer, Colors, Tools, Filters, Windows, and Help. Each menu houses a variety of functions relevant to different editing tasks.

6.   Status   Bar   (Bottom)
The status bar displays useful information such as the image's zoom level, memory usage, and messages about ongoing operations. It also provides hints or tips for the selected tool.

7.   Navigation   and   Dockable   Panels
You can customize the UI by adding or removing panels, also known as docks. Want a histogram or a brush selector easily accessible? You can drag these into the interface and dock them wherever it suits your workflow.

Getting started with GIMP 3 is an exciting journey into the world of image editing and design. With its powerful feature set, flexible interface, and zero cost, GIMP provides an incredible opportunity for anyone — beginner or senior — to explore digital creativity. In the next chapter, we'll dive deeper into customizing your workspace so you can work smarter and more comfortably.

Chapter 2

Customizing Your Workspace

Customizing your workspace is one of the key steps in becoming comfortable and efficient with **GIMP 3**. Whether you're brand new to image editing or a seasoned user, creating a personalized editing environment helps boost creativity and productivity. GIMP's interface is highly flexible, giving you full control over how you arrange your panels, toolbars, and docks. This chapter will walk you through everything you need to know to make GIMP feel like your own.

Panels, Docks, and Toolbars

When you launch GIMP, you're greeted with a clean, default interface. But did you know that nearly every part of this layout can be customized? Let's break it down:

Panels (or Dialogs)

Panels in GIMP refer to individual windows or tabs that display specific types of information — such as layers, brushes, tool options, or color history. Some of the most commonly used panels include:

- **Layers**: Shows the layer stack for your project
- **Tool Options**: Settings related to your selected tool
- **Brushes/Patterns/Gradients**: Shows available options for painting or filling
- **Paths**: Displays vector paths you've created
- **Undo History**: Lets you go back through editing steps

Docks

A *dock* in GIMP is essentially a container for one or more panels. You can stack multiple tabs inside a single dock — for example, Layers, Channels, and Paths can all live in one dock and be accessed by clicking their respective tabs.

To move a panel to a different dock or location:

1. Click and drag the tab of the panel you want to move.
2. Drop it into another dock or into the workspace to create a new dock.
3. If you see a blue highlight while dragging, that's GIMP showing you where the panel will be placed.

You can also remove tabs by clicking the small arrow on the panel tab, then choosing **"Close Tab."**

Toolbars

Toolbars are static sections of the workspace, usually positioned on the left (Toolbox) and top (Main Menu). The **Toolbox** contains frequently-used tools such as Move, Crop, Paintbrush, and more.

You can add or remove tools from the toolbox:

1. Go to **Edit > Preferences > Interface > Toolbox.**
2. Check or uncheck the tools you want visible.
3. Restart GIMP if necessary to apply changes.

Reorganizing your panels and tools lets you remove clutter and make room for the elements you use most. For example, if you never use Paths or Gradients, feel free to close them and expand your Layers and Brushes panels instead.

Saving and Loading Workspaces

Once you've customized GIMP's layout to your liking, you don't want to lose it every time you close the app. Fortunately, GIMP allows you to save your workspace — or even create multiple layouts for different kinds of projects.

Saving Your Custom Workspace Automatically

GIMP usually saves your last-used layout by default. That means any changes you make to the layout (like adding or moving panels) will be remembered the next time you open the program.

But to be sure:

1. Go to **Edit > Preferences > Interface > Window Management.**
2. Make sure **"Save window positions on exit"** is checked.

3. You can also click **"Save Window Positions Now"** to manually save the current state.

Creating Custom Saved Layouts (Session Management)

For more advanced users, it may be helpful to save different layouts for different workflows — such as photo retouching, digital painting, or graphic design.

While GIMP doesn't have named workspace presets like Photoshop, you can save different configuration files and switch between them manually. For most beginners and casual users, saving the last window position is enough.

Restoring the Default Layout

If things get too cluttered or you accidentally close important panels, you can reset the layout:

- Go to **Windows > Dockable Dialogs** to reopen any missing panels.
- Or click **Windows > Single-Window Mode** to simplify the workspace.
- To reset everything, go to **Edit > Preferences > Window Management**

and click "**Reset Saved Window Positions to Default Values.**"

Keyboard Shortcuts for Productivity

GIMP is packed with features, but navigating through menus every time can slow you down. That's where keyboard shortcuts come in — and GIMP lets you customize them to fit your habits and workflow.

Customizing Keyboard Shortcuts

GIMP gives you full control to create or modify shortcuts:

1. Go to **Edit > Keyboard Shortcuts.**
2. Search for a tool or command using the search bar.
3. Click on the action you want to change and press your desired key combo.
4. Conflicting shortcuts will be highlighted, allowing you to resolve them.

Your custom shortcuts will be saved and automatically loaded the next time you open GIMP.

Want to use the same shortcuts on another device or back them up?

- Go to **Edit > Preferences > Interface > Configure Keyboard Shortcuts.**
- Click **Export** to save your custom keymap as a file.
- You can then **Import** it on another machine or after reinstalling GIMP.

This is particularly useful if you prefer Photoshop-style shortcuts or want to standardize your layout across multiple computers.

Customizing your workspace in GIMP 3 is all about making the software work *for you*. Whether it's rearranging panels, simplifying the interface, or using keyboard shortcuts to speed up your workflow, a personalized environment helps you feel more at home and in control. GIMP's flexibility is one of its greatest strengths, and once you've tailored it to your needs, you'll find that editing and designing become not just easier — but also more enjoyable.

Chapter 3

Understanding File Formats and Image Sizes

One of the most important skills in image editing and graphic design is knowing how to work with **file formats** and **image dimensions**. In GIMP 3, understanding these concepts ensures that your final product looks the way you intend—whether it's being posted online, printed on paper, or saved for future editing. In this chapter, we'll explore the most common file formats used in GIMP, how to choose the right resolution for your projects, and how to use tools for scaling, cropping, and adjusting canvas size.

Common Image Formats in GIMP

GIMP supports a wide variety of image file formats, each with its own strengths and best-use scenarios. Choosing the correct format for your project is critical, as it affects image quality, file size, and editability.

1. XCF (GIMP's Native Format)

- **Use when:** You want to keep all editing features (layers, masks, paths).
- **Key benefit:** Saves your work exactly as it is.
- **Limitation:** Not widely supported outside GIMP.

The XCF format is perfect for ongoing projects. Always save a master copy in XCF before exporting to other formats.

2. JPEG (.jpg or .jpeg)

- **Use when:** You need a smaller file size for web or email.
- **Key benefit:** High compression reduces file size.
- **Limitation:** Loss of quality each time it's saved (lossy format), and it doesn't support transparency or layers.

JPEG is great for final images like photos or web content, where file size matters more than preserving every pixel perfectly.

3. PNG (.png)

- **Use when:** You need high quality and transparency.
- **Key benefit:** Lossless compression and supports transparent backgrounds.
- **Limitation:** Larger file size compared to JPEG.

PNG is ideal for logos, illustrations, and graphics that need to maintain sharp edges or have a transparent background.

4. GIF (.gif)

- **Use when:** You want to create basic animations or save simple graphics.
- **Key benefit:** Supports transparency and animations.
- **Limitation:** Limited color range (256 colors max).

GIF is useful for animated stickers or simple web graphics, but not ideal for detailed images or photography.

5. TIFF (.tif or .tiff)

- **Use when:** You need high-quality images for printing or archiving.
- **Key benefit:** Lossless and supports multiple layers (in some apps).
- **Limitation:** Large file size.

TIFF is widely used in professional printing and photography due to its superior quality and fidelity.

6. PSD (.psd)

- **Use when:** You're collaborating with Photoshop users.
- **Key benefit:** Some compatibility with Adobe Photoshop files.
- **Limitation:** May not support all Photoshop features perfectly in GIMP.

While not a perfect substitute, GIMP can open and edit many PSD files, making it possible to work in mixed-software environments.

Choosing the Right Resolution

Resolution plays a big role in image quality. It's measured in **pixels per inch (PPI)** or **dots per**

inch (DPI) and determines how much detail is packed into an image.

For Web and Digital Use:

- Recommended resolution: **72 to 96 PPI**
- Images are optimized for screens and online platforms.
- Lower resolution = smaller file size and faster loading.

For Print Use:

- Recommended resolution: **300 PPI**
- Ensures sharp and professional-quality prints.
- Higher resolution = larger file size but better clarity on paper.

When creating a new project in GIMP:

1. Go to **File > New**.
2. In the "Advanced Options," set the resolution to match your purpose.
3. Choose appropriate width and height based on print size or screen dimensions.

Tip: You can change the resolution of an image later via **Image > Print Size**—but be cautious!

Increasing resolution after the fact may blur or degrade the image.

Scaling, Cropping, and Canvas Sizing

Image dimensions determine how large your image will appear on screen or in print. GIMP offers several tools to modify image size, trim unnecessary elements, or extend your canvas to add more design elements.

Scaling an Image

Scaling changes the overall size (dimensions) of an image.

To scale an image:

1. Go to **Image > Scale Image**.
2. Enter your desired width and height.
3. Make sure the chain icon is linked if you want to maintain the aspect ratio.
4. Choose a quality interpolation method:

   - **Cubic** or **LoHalo** (recommended for photos and smooth scaling)

5. Click **Scale**.

Use Case: Scaling is useful when preparing images for different platforms (e.g., social media, websites, thumbnails).

Cropping an Image

Cropping removes unwanted outer areas of an image to focus on the subject or improve composition.

To crop:

1. Select the **Crop Tool** from the toolbox or press Shift + C.
2. Click and drag over the area you want to keep.
3. Adjust the borders as needed.
4. Press **Enter** to apply the crop.

You can also crop to specific aspect ratios— perfect for creating social media posts, thumbnails, or portrait shots.

Adjusting Canvas Size

Canvas size refers to the space your image sits on. Changing it doesn't scale or crop the image— it adds or removes space around it.

To change canvas size:

1. Go to **Image > Canvas Size**.
2. Enter new dimensions.
3. Use the preview window to reposition the image within the new canvas.
4. Click **Resize**.

Use Case: Expanding the canvas is great when you want to add text, frames, or more design elements without affecting the original image size.

Putting It All Together: A Practical Example

Let's say you've taken a photo that you want to turn into a YouTube thumbnail:

1. **Open your photo** in GIMP.
2. **Crop** it to a 16:9 aspect ratio using the Crop Tool and enable **Fixed Aspect Ratio**.
3. **Scale** the image to 1280x720 pixels, the standard size for HD thumbnails.
4. Add a **transparent text overlay** or logo by exporting the final version as a **PNG**.
5. Save your work in **XCF** format so you can come back later and make changes.

By combining file format knowledge with resolution control and size adjustments, you can ensure that your graphics always look professional and polished.

Mastering file formats and image sizes is an essential step in becoming confident with GIMP 3. Knowing when to use JPEG versus PNG, or how to scale and crop without losing quality, empowers you to create better images—faster. As you become more familiar with these tools, you'll notice that your editing becomes more intentional and your final products look sharper and more professional.

Chapter 4

Essential Tools and What They Do

The true power of GIMP 3 lies in its wide range of creative and functional tools. Whether you're adjusting the position of an image, adding color, drawing freehand, or inserting text, understanding these **essential tools** is key to becoming confident and efficient in your editing process. In this chapter, we'll explore some of the most commonly used tools in GIMP, what they do, and when to use them—perfect for both beginners and seniors looking to master image editing.

Move, Scale, Crop, and Rotate

These four tools fall into the category of **transform tools**—they allow you to reposition, resize, trim, or turn elements in your project. You'll use them frequently for both small tweaks and major layout changes.

Move Tool (M)

The **Move Tool** lets you reposition layers, text, paths, or selections.

How to use:

1. Select the Move Tool from the toolbox (or press M).
2. Click and drag the item you want to move.
3. Choose between moving **layers**, **selections**, or **paths** in the tool options.

Tip: Be sure you have the correct layer selected in the **Layers panel**. If you accidentally move the wrong layer, just press Ctrl + Z to undo.

Scale Tool (Shift + S)

The **Scale Tool** resizes your selected layer, selection, or path.

Steps:

1. Select the Scale Tool.
2. Click on the layer or object to scale.
3. Enter new width and height or drag the handles.
4. Click **Scale** to apply.

Use this tool to shrink or enlarge elements without changing the canvas size.

Crop Tool (Shift + C)

Cropping helps you remove unwanted parts of an image and tighten the composition.

Steps:

1. Activate the Crop Tool.
2. Click and drag to select the area you want to keep.
3. Adjust the corners and press **Enter** to crop.

You can also enable **Fixed Aspect Ratio** to crop to specific dimensions—useful for things like social media banners or photo frames.

Rotate Tool (Shift + R)

The Rotate Tool lets you spin an image, layer, or selection to a desired angle.

How it works:

1. Select the Rotate Tool.
2. Click on the layer or selection to rotate.
3. Enter the angle manually or use the slider.

4. Press **Rotate** to apply.

Bucket Fill, Gradient, and Paint Tools

These tools let you **add color**, **create backgrounds**, and **design illustrations**. They're perfect for both artistic drawing and basic design work.

Bucket Fill Tool (Shift + B)

The Bucket Fill Tool fills an area with a solid color or pattern.

Use it to:

- Color in a closed shape or selection.
- Apply textures using patterns.

Options include:

- **Fill whole selection** or **similar color regions**.
- Use **foreground color**, **background color**, or a **pattern**.

Pro Tip: To prevent unwanted spillover, adjust the **Threshold** setting—higher values include more shades when filling.

Gradient Tool (G)

The Gradient Tool blends two or more colors in a smooth transition. It's great for backgrounds, lighting effects, or artistic designs.

How to use:

1. Select the Gradient Tool.
2. Choose a preset or create your own in the **Tool Options**.
3. Click and drag across your canvas to apply the gradient.

You can control:

- **Shape** (Linear, Radial, Spiral, etc.)
- **Color stops** and **opacity**
- **Blending modes**

Use gradients to add depth or dynamic lighting to your compositions.

Paint Tools

GIMP includes several brush-based tools, each with unique purposes:

Each tool shares common settings such as:

- Brush shape and size
- Opacity
- Hardness
- Flow

These paint tools make GIMP incredibly versatile, from retouching photos to creating digital art from scratch.

Text and Path Tools Explained

Text and paths are essential when working on graphic design projects like posters, banners, or social media content.

Text Tool (T)

The Text Tool allows you to create and format text directly on your image.

Steps:

1. Click the **Text Tool** or press T.
2. Click anywhere on the canvas and start typing.
3. Use the **Tool Options** or the **Floating Toolbar** to change font, size, spacing, color, and alignment.

You can move the text around using the **Move Tool**, and transform it using **Scale**, **Rotate**, and **Perspective** tools.

Text layers remain editable, but if you apply certain filters or merge them with other layers, they become rasterized—no longer editable as text.

Tip: For advanced text effects, combine the Text Tool with layer masks, gradients, or shadows.

Path Tool (B)

The Path Tool is a powerful feature for creating vector-style lines, curves, and selections.

You can use it to:

- Draw custom shapes and curves.
- Create precise selections for cropping or masking.
- Design logos or line art.

Steps:

1. Click to create anchor points.
2. Drag to create curves.

3. Press **Enter** to convert the path into a selection.
4. Use **Edit > Stroke Path** to outline it or **Bucket Fill** to color it in.

The Path Tool can be tricky at first, but with practice, it becomes one of the most flexible tools in GIMP.

Mastering GIMP's essential tools is a huge step toward unlocking your creative potential. From basic tasks like moving and cropping images to more advanced features like gradients, brushwork, and paths, these tools form the foundation of nearly every project you'll undertake in GIMP. Understanding what they do—and when to use them—makes your editing faster, smoother, and more professional.

Chapter 5

Working with Layers

Layers are at the core of what makes GIMP 3 such a powerful and flexible tool for image editing and design. Think of layers like transparent sheets stacked on top of each other—each sheet can hold different elements (like text, images, or effects), and together, they form your final composition.

In this chapter, we'll cover the **basics of layers**, how to use **layer modes and opacity**, and how to manage more complex compositions using **layer groups and masks**. Once you understand how to use layers effectively, your editing workflow will become more non-destructive, organized, and professional.

Introduction to Layers

A **layer** in GIMP is like a separate page or slide in your project. You can paint on it, move it, rotate it, apply effects, or hide it—without affecting other layers.

Key Benefits of Using Layers:

- Keep elements separate for easy editing
- Apply effects and filters to specific parts of an image
- Rearrange or remove objects without starting over
- Maintain flexibility in design and experimentation

When you open or create a new image in GIMP, it usually starts with a **Background layer**. As you add more content—like text, shapes, or pasted images—each item can (and often should) be placed on its own layer.

Working with the Layers Panel

You'll find the **Layers panel** in the dock on the right side of your screen. It shows a list of all the layers in your project from top (visible front) to bottom (background). You can:

- Toggle visibility (eye icon)
- Lock transparency or pixels
- Reorder layers by dragging them
- Rename by double-clicking the layer name

Creating a New Layer:

- Go to **Layer > New from Visible**, or
- Click the **New Layer** button in the Layers panel

When creating a new layer, you can set its dimensions, fill type (transparent, white, or background color), and name. It's good practice to name your layers clearly (e.g., "Logo," "Text Shadow," or "Main Image") to stay organized.

Layer Modes and Opacity

Layer modes (also known as **blending modes**) determine how one layer interacts with the layers beneath it. This allows for creative effects, lighting adjustments, and color blending without altering the original image content.

Layer Opacity

Opacity controls how transparent or solid a layer is:

- **100% opacity** means fully visible.
- **0% opacity** makes the layer invisible.
- Slide the opacity bar in the Layers panel to adjust.

Layer Groups and Masks

As your projects become more complex, managing many layers can become difficult. That's where **layer groups** and **masks** come in.

Layer Groups

A **layer group** allows you to bundle multiple layers together—like putting them into a folder. This is especially useful when working on complex scenes or UI designs where different elements (like buttons, backgrounds, or effects) need to stay organized.

To create a Layer Group:

1. Click the **folder icon** at the bottom of the Layers panel.
2. Drag existing layers into the group.
3. Expand or collapse the group to stay organized.

Benefits:

- Move or scale grouped elements together
- Apply the same mask or transform to multiple layers
- Keep your workspace clean and structured

Layer Masks

A **layer mask** is a grayscale image that controls which parts of a layer are visible. This allows you to **hide or reveal** parts of a layer without permanently deleting anything—making it a powerful non-destructive editing tool.

White areas on a mask = visible
Black areas = hidden
Gray = partial transparency

How to Add a Layer Mask:

1. Right-click a layer > **Add Layer Mask**
2. Choose **White (full opacity)** to begin with a fully visible layer
3. Select the mask thumbnail in the Layers panel
4. Use the **Paintbrush Tool**:

- Paint with **black** to hide
- Paint with **white** to reveal
- Use **gray** for partial transparency

Common uses for layer masks:

- Blending two photos together
- Fading edges of an image

- Creating soft shadows or light effects
- Selectively applying filters or adjustments

Tip: You can disable a mask temporarily by right-clicking it and selecting **Disable Layer Mask,** allowing you to compare the masked and unmasked view.

Practical Example: Creating a Simple Poster Design

Let's walk through how layers come together in a real-world example.

1. **Background Layer**: Use a gradient fill or an image.
2. **Main Subject Layer**: Add a cut-out photo on top.
3. **Text Layer**: Use the Text Tool for a catchy headline.
4. **Shadow Layer**: Duplicate the subject, fill it black, lower the opacity, and blur.
5. **Overlay Layer**: Add texture and change the layer mode to Overlay.
6. **Logo Group**: Include multiple logo elements grouped together.

Use **layer masks** to subtly blend your subject into the background and **adjust opacity** to make the text feel integrated with the design. The entire poster can be adjusted, refined, or exported without ever flattening your layers—thanks to GIMP's powerful layer system.

Layers are the foundation of advanced image editing in GIMP 3. Whether you're building a simple collage or working on a complex multi-element design, learning how to organize, blend, and mask your layers gives you maximum flexibility and creative control. From opacity and layer modes to groups and masks, mastering these techniques will transform your workflow and results.

In the next chapter, we'll dive into **selections and masks**—how to isolate specific parts of your image for targeted editing.

Chapter 6

Selections and Masks

Selections are one of the most powerful tools in image editing because they allow you to **isolate specific areas** of your image for targeted changes. Whether you're adjusting color, cutting out objects, or applying effects, selections give you **precision control** over your work.

Rectangle, Ellipse, and Free Select

GIMP provides several tools to make selections in different shapes and forms, depending on the image and your goals.

Rectangle Select Tool (R)

This tool allows you to create rectangular selections with ease—perfect for cropping, framing, or isolating geometric areas.

To use:

1. Click on the **Rectangle Select Tool** from the toolbox or press R.

2. Click and drag on the canvas to create your rectangle.
3. Adjust size and position using the handles.
4. Press **Enter** to confirm the selection.

Tool options let you:

- Fix aspect ratio (useful for photos)
- Round corners
- Expand from center

Ellipse Select Tool (E)

The Ellipse Select Tool lets you make oval or circular selections—useful for highlighting faces, making badges, or applying vignettes.

To use:

1. Select the **Ellipse Tool** or press E.
2. Click and drag to draw an ellipse.
3. Adjust and position it as needed.

As with the rectangle tool, you can fix aspect ratios or expand from the center.

Free Select Tool (F)

The Free Select Tool (also called the Lasso Tool) gives you full control to draw **custom shapes**—

either by clicking points (polygonal selection) or drawing freehand.

Steps:

1. Activate the tool and begin clicking around the object to create a selection outline.
2. Close the loop by clicking back on the first point or pressing **Enter**.
3. The area inside becomes the active selection.

Pro Tip: You can switch between straight lines and freehand drawing by clicking and dragging.

Quick Mask Mode

Sometimes, using selection tools alone isn't enough—especially when you're working with complex shapes like hair, fabric, or smoke. That's where **Quick Mask Mode** shines.

Quick Mask lets you **paint your selection** using brushes, giving you total freedom and accuracy.

Activating Quick Mask

- Click the **small square icon** at the bottom-left of the image window, or press Shift + Q.

You'll notice the image is overlaid with a **red mask**—this represents areas that are *not* selected.

How it works:

- Paint with **black** to exclude areas from the selection.
- Paint with **white** to include areas in the selection.
- Use shades of **gray** for partial selections (soft edges).

Use any brush, size, or shape to paint in the Quick Mask—this is incredibly helpful for detailed work like isolating a person from a background.

When you're done:

- Press Shift + Q again to exit Quick Mask mode.
- Your brush-painted selection becomes active, ready for editing or masking.

Refining Selections

Once you've made a basic selection, you'll often need to **fine-tune the edges** to make them cleaner and more natural. GIMP offers several ways to do this.

Feathering Selections

Feathering softens the edges of a selection, which is especially useful when blending two images together or making subtle adjustments.

To apply feathering:

- Go to **Select > Feather**
- Choose how many pixels to soften

This makes the selection edges blend more smoothly with the surrounding area.

Grow and Shrink

Need to make a selection slightly larger or smaller?

- **Select > Grow** expands the selection outward.
- **Select > Shrink** pulls the edges inward.

This is handy for fitting borders or avoiding unwanted halos when cutting out objects.

Border

Creates a selection in the shape of a border (like a ring) from an existing selection.

Steps:

- Go to **Select > Border**
- Enter pixel width for the border thickness

Perfect for creating stylized effects or outlines.

Select by Color Tool (Shift + O)

Want to select all pixels of a specific color? Use the **Select by Color Tool**.

Steps:

1. Activate the tool.
2. Click on the color in the image.
3. Adjust the **Threshold** to include more or fewer similar tones.

This is excellent for removing solid-colored backgrounds or adjusting uniformly colored areas.

Fuzzy Select Tool (U)

Also known as the "Magic Wand," this tool selects adjacent pixels of similar color.

Use it when:

- You want to quickly isolate a single colored object.
- You're working with simple backgrounds or designs.

Adjust the **Threshold** in the tool options to make the selection more or less sensitive.

Refine Edges Manually

For the highest control, you can:

- Switch to **Quick Mask** for brush-based adjustments.
- Use **Layer Masks** for non-destructive cleanup.
- Zoom in and tweak with the **Lasso Tool**.

You can also invert selections (**Select > Invert**) to quickly switch focus from object to background—or vice versa.

Practical Example: Cutting Out a Subject

Let's say you want to remove the background from a photo of a person:

1. Use the **Free Select Tool** to outline the person roughly.
2. Switch to **Quick Mask Mode** and refine the edges with a soft brush.
3. Exit Quick Mask and apply **Feather** for smooth transition.
4. Invert the selection, then press Delete or add a **Layer Mask** to remove the background.

You now have a clean cut-out of the person, ready to place into a new background or composite image.

Selections and masks are foundational to precise and professional image editing. With tools like rectangle, ellipse, and free select for general shapes, and the powerful Quick Mask mode for detailed adjustments, you gain full control over your workflow. Refining selections with feathering, color tools, and manual touch-ups ensures that your edits look seamless and polished.

Chapter 7

Color and Tone Adjustments

One of the most important aspects of image editing is adjusting **color and tone** to bring out the best in your photos or designs. Whether you're correcting a poorly lit image, adding creative flair, or just enhancing vibrancy, GIMP 3 offers a variety of powerful tools to get the job done.

Brightness, Contrast, and Levels

The first step in many editing workflows is fixing exposure and bringing out detail in your image. GIMP provides simple but effective tools for this.

Brightness and Contrast

This is the most basic adjustment tool, but still incredibly useful.

Steps:

1. Go to **Colors > Brightness-Contrast**
2. Move the sliders:

- **Brightness** makes the entire image lighter or darker
- **Contrast** increases or decreases the difference between light and dark areas

This is ideal for quick fixes or enhancing a washed-out or flat image.

Tip: Try small adjustments—overdoing contrast can lead to loss of detail in shadows and highlights.

Levels

Levels give you more control over the tonal range of your image by letting you adjust the shadows, midtones, and highlights independently.

Access it via: Colors > Levels

In the **Levels dialog**, you'll see a histogram—a graph showing how tones are distributed in your image.

Key sliders:

- **Black point (left):** Sets the darkest value
- **Midtone (middle):** Adjusts overall brightness

- **White point (right):** Sets the lightest value

How to use:

1. Drag the black and white sliders inward to where the data starts.
2. Adjust the midtone to brighten or darken the mid-range.

You can also adjust **individual RGB channels** (Red, Green, Blue) to fix color balance issues or create stylized effects.

Hue, Saturation, and Color Balance

Once the exposure looks good, the next step is enhancing or correcting the **colors** in your image. GIMP offers intuitive tools to do this efficiently.

Hue-Saturation

This tool allows you to control the intensity and tint of the colors in your image.

Open via: Colors > Hue-Saturation

Sliders:

- **Hue:** Shifts all colors around the color wheel (useful for creative changes)
- **Lightness:** Brightens or darkens the colors
- **Saturation:** Controls how vivid the colors are

You can also target specific color ranges (e.g., adjust only blues or reds) for more precise corrections.

Use cases:

- Boost colors in a dull photo
- Change the color of an object (e.g., red shirt to green)
- Create a vintage or monochrome look

Color Balance

This tool is designed for correcting **color casts** or creating a particular mood or atmosphere.

Open via: Colors > Color Balance

It lets you adjust the mix of red, green, and blue in **shadows**, **midtones**, and **highlights** separately.

Use cases:

- Fix photos that look too blue (cool) or too yellow (warm)
- Add a cinematic tone by shifting shadows and highlights
- Enhance sunset scenes with richer reds and oranges

Pro Tip: Always evaluate changes on a calibrated monitor or with a neutral background to avoid biased perception.

Using Curves and Threshold

For finer control over tone and contrast, GIMP's **Curves** tool is incredibly powerful, and **Threshold** offers creative possibilities for high-contrast effects.

Curves

Curves allow you to manipulate the brightness and contrast across the tonal spectrum using a graph-based interface.

Open via: Colors > Curves

You'll see a diagonal line from the bottom-left (shadows) to the top-right (highlights). By adding points and adjusting the curve, you can:

- Brighten highlights
- Deepen shadows
- Add contrast to midtones
- Create custom lighting effects

Common curve shapes:

- **S-curve:** Adds contrast and punch
- **Inverted S:** Softens the image
- **Diagonal shifts:** Change overall brightness

You can also adjust each RGB channel individually to correct color issues or create stylized tints.

Threshold

This tool converts your image into pure **black and white** by cutting off midtones. It's especially useful for:

- Creating high-contrast posters or artwork
- Tracing outlines
- Preparing images for stencils or screen printing

Access it via: Colors > Threshold

How to use:

1. Drag the sliders to choose a cutoff point.
2. Everything below becomes black; above becomes white.

Tip: Combine Threshold with **selection masks** or **layer blending modes** to mix dramatic black-and-white elements into color designs.

Workflow Example: Color Correction for a Portrait

Let's walk through a basic color and tone adjustment workflow for a portrait image:

1. **Levels**: Use the histogram to set black and white points for good contrast.
2. **Brightness/Contrast**: Make subtle adjustments to balance the light.
3. **Color Balance**: Remove color cast from indoor lighting by adding blue and reducing yellow.
4. **Hue-Saturation**: Slightly boost skin tones while muting background colors.
5. **Curves**: Add a gentle S-curve to increase depth and drama.
6. **Final Polish**: Use **Layer Masks** to apply adjustments selectively, like boosting brightness only on the face.

Tips for Better Color Editing in GIMP:

- **Use adjustment layers:** While GIMP doesn't have traditional adjustment layers like Photoshop, you can simulate them by duplicating layers and applying changes with layer masks.
- **Work in 16-bit color when possible** for better detail retention (especially when using curves or multiple edits).
- **Check histograms** after adjustments to avoid clipping highlights or shadows.
- **Zoom out regularly** to see how edits look at a normal viewing size.

Mastering color and tone adjustments in GIMP 3 will dramatically improve the quality and impact of your images. From quick brightness fixes to complex color grading, tools like **Levels, Curves, Hue-Saturation, and Color Balance** give you full control over how your image feels and communicates. With practice, these tools will become second nature, enabling you to bring any photo or design to life.

Chapter 8

Retouching and Photo Corrections

Retouching is where the magic of photo editing often begins—correcting flaws, enhancing details, and transforming ordinary images into polished masterpieces. Whether you're fixing blemishes, restoring old photos, or preparing a portrait for a professional presentation, GIMP 3 equips you with an impressive suite of tools.

Healing, Clone, and Smudge Tools

These tools are your best friends when it comes to fixing imperfections, removing unwanted elements, and blending textures seamlessly.

Healing Tool (Shortcut: H)

The **Healing Tool** is designed for removing blemishes, wrinkles, dust, and other small imperfections by blending the sampled area with the surrounding texture.

How it works:

1. Select the Healing Tool.
2. Hold Ctrl and click to sample a clean area.
3. Paint over the imperfection. GIMP blends the sampled pixels into the painted area.

Best used for:

- Skin retouching (e.g., acne, scars)
- Removing dust from scanned images
- Blending small inconsistencies in textures

Tip: Use a soft-edged brush and zoom in for more precise control.

Clone Tool (Shortcut: C)

Unlike the Healing Tool, the **Clone Tool** directly copies pixels from one area to another. It's more precise and doesn't blend as much, making it ideal for duplicating patterns or removing larger objects.

Steps:

1. Activate the Clone Tool.
2. Ctrl + Click to set the source point.
3. Paint over the area you want to replace.

Use cases:

- Removing people or objects from backgrounds
- Filling in missing parts of an image
- Copying detailed textures (e.g., repeating brick walls)

Pro Tip: Adjust brush hardness and opacity to control the strength of the cloning.

Smudge Tool

The **Smudge Tool** works like dragging your finger across wet paint—it smears pixels to create blended or distorted effects.

Access it via Toolbox or under Paint Tools.

Use cases:

- Softening hard lines or edges
- Creating abstract or artistic effects
- Smoothing skin or blending colors

Be careful with the Smudge Tool—it can easily make things look messy if overused. Combine with layer masks or work on duplicates for safety.

Red-Eye Removal

Red-eye is a common problem in flash photography, where the camera flash reflects off the subject's retina, creating a bright red glow. GIMP makes fixing this quick and easy.

Manual Method:

1. **Zoom in** on the eyes.
2. Use the **Ellipse Select Tool** to select the red areas in each eye.
3. Go to **Colors > Hue-Saturation**

- Select **Reds** from the color channel dropdown.
- Lower the **Saturation** to remove the red color.
- Adjust **Lightness** and **Hue** slightly if needed.

GIMP Plugin Option:

Some versions of GIMP support plug-ins or scripts specifically for red-eye removal (e.g., Red Eye Removal under **Filters > Enhance**). If installed, these tools automate the process.

Noise Reduction and Sharpening

Digital noise—those unwanted specks of color or grain—can creep into your photos, especially in low light or high ISO settings. GIMP provides tools to reduce noise while preserving detail. Once noise is under control, sharpening can help bring back clarity and focus.

Noise Reduction

Option 1: Reduce Noise Filter

- Go to **Filters > Noise > Reduce Noise**
- Adjust the **Strength**, **Preserve Details**, and **Sharpen Edges** sliders
- Preview the effect and apply

Option 2: Selective Gaussian Blur

- Use **Filters > Blur > Selective Gaussian Blur**
- This smooths out noisy areas while retaining edges better than a standard blur.

Pro Tip: Apply noise reduction **before sharpening**, and only to the parts of the image that need it (e.g., shadows or background).

Once your photo is cleaned up, sharpening brings back the crispness that might've been lost during noise reduction or resizing.

Option 1: Unsharp Mask

- Found under **Filters > Enhance > Unsharp Mask**
- Despite its name, it sharpens by increasing contrast at edges.

Settings to try:

- **Radius:** How far the sharpening effect spreads
- **Amount:** How strong the sharpening is
- **Threshold:** Controls which pixels get sharpened (higher = less sharpening)

This method gives you fine control and works well for portraits and detailed scenes.

Option 2: High Pass Filter Method (Advanced)

1. Duplicate your image layer.

2. Apply **High Pass Filter** (via plug-in or manual method using Filters > Enhance > High Pass).
3. Set the duplicate layer's blend mode to **Overlay** or **Soft Light.**

Workflow Example: Retouching a Portrait

Here's how you might retouch a simple headshot using GIMP 3:

1. **Duplicate the original layer**: Always work non-destructively.
2. Use the **Healing Tool** to clean up skin blemishes.
3. Use the **Clone Tool** to remove distracting background elements.
4. Zoom in and remove **red-eye** using manual hue adjustment.
5. Apply **Reduce Noise** filter to smooth out grain.
6. Add **Unsharp Mask** to enhance clarity in the eyes and hair.
7. Optionally, use **Smudge Tool** to blend skin or background transitions.

Always compare your final image with the original to ensure you haven't gone too far—natural results are key.

Tips for Effective Retouching:

- **Work on duplicates** or use **layer masks** to keep edits reversible.
- **Zoom in and out often** to check both detail and full-image impact.
- **Use a graphics tablet** for better brush control if available.
- **Keep skin texture intact**: Over-smoothing can make subjects look artificial.
- **Sharpen selectively**: Not every part of the image needs enhancement.

Retouching in GIMP 3 is a powerful way to improve and personalize your photos. With tools like Healing, Clone, and Smudge, combined with red-eye fixes, noise control, and sharpening, you can dramatically enhance image quality. These techniques are not just for professionals—anyone can learn them and apply them with practice and patience.

Chapter 9

Text and Typography in GIMP

Adding text to your graphics is essential for everything from branding and posters to memes and professional design work. GIMP 3 makes it easy to incorporate text into your images, whether you're adding simple labels or creating complex stylized typography.

Adding and Editing Text

GIMP's text tool allows you to insert, edit, and manipulate text with flexibility and precision. It functions similarly to text tools in other design programs but offers extra control for pixel-level editing.

How to Add Text:

1. Select the **Text Tool** from the Toolbox or press T.
2. Click on the canvas where you want the text to appear.
3. A text box will appear. Start typing your desired content.

4. Use the **Tool Options** panel below the Toolbox to adjust:

- Font type
- Font size
- Text alignment
- Line and letter spacing
- Color

Each time you add text, GIMP creates a **dedicated text layer**. This is editable at any time—just double-click on the layer or use the **Text Tool** to select it again.

Editing Text:

- Select the text layer from the **Layers panel**.
- Use the **Text Tool** to change the wording or formatting.
- To move the text, switch to the **Move Tool** and drag it to a new position.

Tip: Keep text on separate layers if you're creating multiple headings or captions—this offers more layout control.

Using Fonts and Custom Styles

Typography isn't just about what you say—it's how it looks. Choosing the right font and styling your text gives your message personality, professionalism, or visual impact.

Changing Fonts in GIMP:

- With the text layer active and the **Text Tool** selected, go to the **Tool Options** and pick a font from the dropdown list.
- You can type the font name for faster searching.

GIMP supports all fonts installed on your system, including **custom fonts**.

Customizing Styles:

Once you've selected a font, you can enhance it using:

- **Bold, Italic, and Underline** (available in Tool Options)
- **Kerning** (space between characters)
- **Line Spacing** (distance between lines of text)

- **Text Color** (via the color selector in Tool Options)

Styling Tip:

To apply different styles (e.g., bold for one word) within a single text box:

1. Highlight the text you want to modify.
2. Apply formatting directly from the Tool Options or right-click for more choices.

You can also fill text with gradients or patterns using **Alpha to Selection** and **Bucket Fill** on the text layer.

Text Effects and Text Along Paths

For more creative typography, GIMP lets you add visual effects and even wrap text around curves and shapes.

Basic Text Effects:

Some quick and fun ways to make your text pop include:

1. **Drop Shadows**

- Go to **Filters** > **Light and Shadow** > **Drop Shadow**
- Adjust blur, offset, and color for depth

2. **Outline Text**

- Right-click on the text layer > **Alpha to Selection**
- Go to **Select** > **Grow** (increase by a few pixels)
- Create a new layer, then fill the selection with a color using the **Bucket Fill Tool**

3. **Gradient Fill**

- Use **Alpha to Selection** on the text layer
- Select the **Gradient Tool**
- Drag the gradient across the selected text area

4. **Bevel or Emboss**

- Use **Filters** > **Decor** > **Add Bevel**
- This adds depth and makes the text look raised

Text Along Paths

Want to bend text along a curve or circle? GIMP makes it possible using paths.

Step-by-Step Guide:

1. **Create a Path:**

   - Use the **Paths Tool (B)** to draw your curve
   - Click to add points, and drag to curve the line

2. **Add Your Text:**

   - Use the **Text Tool** to type your content

3. **Text to Path:**

   - With the text layer active, right-click and choose **Text Along Path**
   - This creates a new path layer that follows the shape of your original curve

4. **Stroke the Path:**

   - Make a new transparent layer
   - Go to **Edit > Stroke Path**, select line width and style

- You now have curved text drawn onto your canvas

Tip: You can fill the path with colors or gradients for more visual flair.

Workflow Example: Creating a Poster Title

Here's a simple typography workflow for a poster heading:

1. Create a large, bold text layer with the **Text Tool**.
2. Apply a **Drop Shadow** using Filters.
3. Use **Alpha to Selection** and add an **Outline** layer behind the text.
4. Apply a **Gradient Fill** inside the text for a colorful effect.
5. Add a **Bevel Filter** to make it pop.
6. (Optional) Curve the subtitle text **along a path** to wrap it around a graphic element.

This combination produces professional-looking typography suitable for flyers, ads, and digital media.

Tips for Better Typography in GIMP:

- **Use contrasting fonts** (e.g., serif + sans-serif) for visual balance.
- **Don't overcrowd your layout**: Give text room to breathe.
- **Limit font styles**: 1 or 2 fonts per project is often best.
- **Align text consistently** using GIMP's **Align Tool** or guides.
- **Use layer groups** to organize complex text designs (e.g., headings, subheadings, captions).

Text and typography in GIMP 3 offer limitless design possibilities, whether you're crafting sleek headers, designing logos, or wrapping messages around shapes. With tools for basic text editing and advanced styling techniques like curved text and shadowing, you can turn simple text into powerful design elements.

Chapter 10

Drawing and Painting with GIMP

While GIMP is often seen as a powerful photo-editing tool, it's also a capable digital painting and drawing platform. Whether you're sketching, painting vibrant illustrations, or adding hand-drawn touches to photos, GIMP 3 provides a robust set of tools to unleash your creativity.

Brush Basics and Custom Brushes

At the heart of GIMP's drawing and painting features is its **brush system**. Brushes define the shape and texture of the strokes you paint on the canvas.

Accessing the Brush Tool Options:

Every painting tool (Pencil, Paintbrush, Airbrush, Clone, etc.) uses a brush. You can select brushes from the **Tool Options** or the

Brush Dialog (Windows > Dockable Dialogs > Brushes).

Types of Brushes:

GIMP includes several default brushes:

- Hard or soft round brushes (good for general use)
- Textured brushes (simulate pencils, chalk, etc.)
- Patterned brushes (used for stamps and effects)

Each brush has customizable properties:

- Size
- Aspect ratio
- Angle
- Spacing

You can adjust these in the Tool Options or through **Dynamics** settings for more advanced control.

Creating Custom Brushes:

1. **Start with a new canvas** and design your brush shape (black shapes work best).

2. **Save it as a .gbr file** (GIMP Brush File).
3. Move it to your GIMP brushes folder:
4. Reload brushes via the **Brush Dialog**.

Pencil, Paintbrush, and Airbrush

Each of these tools offers unique characteristics, giving you full creative control depending on the effect you're going for.

Pencil Tool (Shortcut: N)

The Pencil Tool draws **hard-edged**, pixel-precise lines. It's great for:

- Pixel art
- Crisp outlines
- Rough sketching

Since it doesn't anti-alias, the Pencil is perfect when you want sharp transitions and a retro aesthetic.

Settings to adjust:

- Brush type (choose a square or hard round for precise pixels)
- Size and spacing
- Opacity

Paintbrush Tool (Shortcut: P)

The Paintbrush Tool is your go-to for **soft strokes**, blending, and smooth transitions. It supports all brush types and dynamics.

Best used for:

- Painting and shading
- Blending colors
- Smooth, organic strokes

You can simulate pressure by adjusting the **Fade**, **Jitter**, or using input dynamics (if you have a graphics tablet).

Airbrush Tool (Shortcut: A)

The Airbrush Tool simulates **spray painting**, gradually applying color based on how long you hold down your mouse button or stylus.

Ideal for:

- Building up color gradually
- Light shading
- Creating spray-paint textures

Adjust **Rate** and **Pressure** to control the effect. It's slower than the Paintbrush but useful for subtle tonal variations.

Dynamic Painting Techniques

Dynamic painting lets you simulate real-world drawing behavior like pen pressure, tilt, speed, and randomness—even with a mouse. These features become even more powerful if you're using a graphics tablet.

Using Dynamics:

In the **Tool Options**, look for the **"Dynamics"** dropdown. Choose a preset like:

- **Basic Dynamics**: Adds pressure sensitivity (for tablet users)
- **Color from Gradient**: Paints with a gradient instead of solid color
- **Opacity and Size Jitter**: Randomizes stroke thickness and opacity
- **Velocity Tapering**: Changes stroke thickness based on speed

You can also create your **own custom dynamics**:

1. Open **Windows** > **Dockable Dialogs** > **Dynamics**.
2. Click the + **icon** to create a new dynamic preset.
3. Assign controls like **Pressure** > **Size, Tilt** > **Opacity**, etc.

Blending and Shading Tips:

- Use **soft brushes** and **low opacity** for gentle blending.
- Build color gradually using the **Airbrush Tool** or **lowered Paintbrush opacity**.
- To blend colors manually, use the **Smudge Tool** or alternate painting between two colors with varying opacity.

Simulating Brush Pressure Without a Tablet:

Even without a stylus, you can fake pressure sensitivity:

- Use **Fade Length** (Tool Options) to taper strokes
- Apply **Size Jitter** from Dynamics
- Manually adjust brush size during painting

Workflow Example: Digital Sketch and Color

Let's say you're sketching a digital character design:

1. **Sketch Layer:** Use the **Pencil Tool** with a small hard brush to rough out the character.
2. **Inking Layer:** Switch to the **Paintbrush Tool** with a soft round brush for clean linework.
3. **Color Layer:** Add a layer below and use the Paintbrush to fill in flat colors.
4. **Shading Layer:** Use the **Airbrush Tool** with low opacity to softly shade the form.
5. **Highlight Layer:** Add pops of light using white with a soft brush and low opacity.

Helpful Painting Tips:

- **Use Layers**: Keep lines, colors, and effects on separate layers.
- **Label Your Layers**: Avoid confusion in complex compositions.
- **Use Layer Masks** for non-destructive shading or adjustments.
- **Experiment with Blending Modes** (like Multiply, Overlay) for different effects.
- **Save Custom Brushes and Dynamics** for consistent results across projects.

Chapter 11

Creating Graphics and Illustrations

While GIMP is well-known for photo editing and digital painting, it's also a powerful platform for creating graphics and illustrations. Whether you're designing a logo, drawing vector-style icons, or composing complex illustrations, GIMP 3 offers a suite of tools that enable clean, scalable, and precise artwork.

In this chapter, you'll learn to use **vector tools and paths**, organize your workspace with **guides and grids**, and master **shapes and strokes** for graphic creation.

Vector Tools and Paths

Although GIMP is primarily a raster-based program (meaning it works with pixels), it includes **vector-like tools**—most notably, the **Paths Tool**—that allow for scalable and editable outlines.

The Paths Tool (Shortcut: B):

The Paths Tool is used to create precise lines and curves which can later be stroked, filled, or converted into selections.

How to Use:

1. Select the **Paths Tool**.
2. Click on the canvas to create **anchor points**.
3. Click and drag to create **curved segments**.
4. Complete the path by pressing Enter or clicking the starting point again.
5. In the **Tool Options**, you can:

- Edit nodes
- Move segments
- Add or delete points

Stroking and Filling Paths:

After creating a path:

- Go to **Edit > Stroke Path** to draw an outline using a brush or solid line.
- Go to **Edit > Fill Path** to fill the enclosed area with color or pattern.

- You can also right-click the path in the
  Paths Dialog for more options.

Converting Paths to Selections:

Paths can be turned into selections for more
controlled editing:

- Right-click the path in the Paths Dialog
  and choose **Path to Selection**.
- Or use the **Selection from Path** button in
  the Tool Options.

This is especially useful when creating
symmetrical designs, logos, or reusable shapes.

Using Guides and Grids

When precision matters—like in UI design,
infographic layout, or symmetrical art—**guides
and grids** can make your work more accurate
and efficient.

Guides:

Guides are non-printing lines you can drag from
the rulers to help align objects.

How to Use:

- Click and drag from the **top or left ruler** onto the canvas.
- To move a guide, use the **Move Tool** and drag it into position.
- To remove, drag it off-canvas or right-click and choose **Remove Guide**.

Aligning Objects to Guides: Enable **Snap to Guides** under **View > Snap to Guides** to have elements automatically align to them.

Grids:

Grids provide a full overlay across the canvas, dividing it into even squares.

Enable Grid:

- Go to **View > Show Grid**.
- Customize under **Image > Configure Grid**—change spacing, color, and line style.

Grids are perfect for:

- Pixel art
- Technical illustrations

- Even spacing of elements

You can also snap elements to the grid by enabling **View > Snap to Grid**.

Working with Shapes and Strokes

While GIMP doesn't have a dedicated shape tool like some vector programs, it still allows you to **create and manipulate shapes** using the **Selection Tools**, **Paths**, and **Stroking**.

Creating Basic Shapes:

Rectangles and Ellipses:

- Use the **Rectangle Select Tool (R)** or **Ellipse Select Tool (E)**.
- In Tool Options, adjust:
- Rounded corners (for rectangles)
- Fixed aspect ratio or size
- Once the shape is selected, fill it with color using the **Bucket Fill Tool (Shift + B)** or **Edit > Fill with FG/BG Color**.

Custom Shapes:

- Use the **Free Select Tool (Lasso)** or **Paths Tool** to create irregular shapes.

- Stroke or fill selections for outlines or solid shapes.

Stroking Shapes:

To add outlines to shapes:

1. Make a selection (rectangle, ellipse, or path).
2. Go to **Edit > Stroke Selection** or **Edit > Stroke Path**.
3. Choose:

- Stroke line (solid or dashed)
- Use a paint tool (e.g., current brush settings)
- Set width and style

This gives your shapes clean edges and stylized outlines.

Workflow Example: Creating a Simple Badge Logo

Let's walk through a quick design using the tools we've covered.

1. **Set Up the Canvas:** Open a new file (e.g., 1000x1000 px). Enable **Grid** for

alignment (View > Show Grid and Snap to Grid).

2. **Draw the Outer Shape:** Use the **Ellipse Select Tool** to make a perfect circle. Fill it with a color. Use **Edit > Stroke Selection** to add an outer ring.

3. **Add Decorative Elements**

- Use **Paths Tool** to create curved lines or abstract shapes.
- Stroke with a dashed line for texture.

4. **Insert Text**

- Add text layers with your company name or message.
- Use **Text Along Path** for circular or curved text.

5. **Refine with Guides**

- Add horizontal and vertical guides to keep elements centered.
- Use the **Align Tool** to position everything neatly.

6. **Final Touches:** Add highlights or shadows with **Brush Tool** and **Opacity adjustments**.

This method allows you to create clean, professional-looking graphics without ever needing to leave GIMP.

Tips for Effective Graphic Design in GIMP:

- **Use Layers Wisely:** Keep each shape, text element, and decoration on a separate layer for easy editing.
- **Label Everything:** Naming your layers helps when projects become complex.
- **Use Paths for Precision:** Especially helpful for icon design or symmetrical shapes.
- **Combine Selection Tools:** Create compound shapes by intersecting or subtracting selections.
- **Save Frequently:** Use .XCF files to retain all layer and path data.

GIMP 3 may be raster-based, but its powerful **path tools**, **guides**, **grids**, and **selection-driven shapes** make it incredibly capable for graphic design and illustration work. Whether you're designing logos, icons, or creative layouts, GIMP gives you precision, flexibility, and creative control.

In the next chapter, we'll dive into **applying filters and effects**, turning your basic graphics and photos into stylized, eye-catching designs with just a few clicks.

Chapter 12

Filters and Effects

One of the most exciting parts of working in GIMP 3 is experimenting with **filters and effects**. Filters allow you to transform your images or artwork with just a few clicks—adding drama, enhancing clarity, simulating textures, or even mimicking classic art styles.

Whether you're a beginner or a seasoned designer, mastering GIMP's filters can unlock a new dimension of creativity. In this chapter, we'll cover **artistic filters, blur, distort, and enhance effects**, and how to **combine filters** for unique, professional-looking results.

Artistic Filters

GIMP's **Artistic Filters** simulate traditional media techniques and creative visual styles. You'll find them under **Filters > Artistic**. These are great for turning photos into paintings, drawings, or stylized illustrations.

Here are some favorites:

1. Cartoon:

- Creates a black outline around edges and simplifies colors.
- Great for comic-style images or turning photos into toons.

How to Use:

- Go to **Filters > Artistic > Cartoon**.
- Adjust the **mask radius** and **percent black** for the desired effect.

2. Oilify:

- Makes an image look like it's been painted with oil on canvas.
- Smoothens textures while retaining color shapes.

How to Use:

- **Filters > Artistic > Oilify**.
- Set the **mask size** to control stroke size.

3. Van Gogh (LIC):

- Adds swirling strokes based on lightness or gradient direction.
- It's inspired by the painter Van Gogh and gives a dreamy effect.

Tip: This filter works best when combined with duplicates of the base image to soften the impact.

4. Softglow:

- Adds a glow around bright areas.
- Ideal for dreamy portraits or fantasy scenes.

Settings to tweak:

- Glow radius
- Brightness
- Sharpness

These artistic filters are perfect for adding stylized touches to your projects, even if you don't consider yourself a painter or illustrator.

Blur, Distort, and Enhance Effects

Sometimes subtlety is key. GIMP offers a wide range of **blurs**, **distortions**, and **enhancements** that allow you to polish your work, simulate lens effects, or correct imperfections.

Blur Effects (Filters > Blur):

1. Gaussian Blur:

- Softens the entire image or selected areas.
- Perfect for smoothing skin, creating soft backgrounds, or enhancing depth of field.

Pro Tip: Duplicate your layer first, blur it, and reduce the opacity to maintain some original detail.

2. Motion Blur:

- Creates a streaked effect, like an object moving rapidly.
- Choose from **Linear**, **Radial**, or **Zoom** blurs.

3. Pixelize:

- Turns your image into blocks of color.
- Good for censoring or creating pixel art effects.

Distort Effects (Filters > Distorts):

1. Ripple:

- Makes your image look like it's been reflected in water.
- Control **amplitude** and **period** for different ripple effects.

2. Lens Distortion:

- Simulates fisheye or barrel lens effects.
- Useful for photo correction or fun exaggeration.

3. Whirl and Pinch:

- Twists and pulls your image around a center point.
- Great for abstract art or surreal distortions.

4. Mosaic:

- Breaks the image into glass-like chunks.
- Gives a stained-glass or shattered effect.

Enhance Effects (Filters > Enhance):

These are useful for **cleaning up** and **refining** images.

1. Unsharp Mask:

- Increases perceived sharpness by enhancing edge contrast.
- Use sparingly to avoid unnatural looks.

2. Noise Reduction:

- Removes graininess or compression artifacts from photos.
- Located under **Filters > Noise > Reduce Noise**.

3. Despeckle:

- Cleans up small specks and spots—especially useful for scanned documents.

4. Red Eye Removal:

- Found under **Filters > Enhance > Red Eye Removal**.
- Automatically detects and removes red-eye effects from flash photography.

Combining Filters for Unique Results

The real power of GIMP's filters comes when you **combine them**. Layering filters and adjusting their intensity allows you to create custom styles that are uniquely yours.

Example Workflow: Dreamy Portrait Look

1. **Duplicate the original layer.**
2. Apply **Gaussian Blur** to the top layer.
3. Set the **layer mode to Soft Light** or **Overlay**.
4. Adjust **opacity** for subtle glow.
5. Add **Filters > Artistic > Softglow** to enhance light spots.
6. Use **Curves** or **Color Balance** to fine-tune the color tone.

Example Workflow: Grunge Poster Effect

1. Convert photo to grayscale.
2. Use **Threshold** or **Posterize** for high-contrast edges.
3. Apply **Filters > Edge-Detect > Difference of Gaussians** for a gritty outline.
4. Add **Noise (RGB or HSV)** to simulate texture.
5. Overlay a concrete or paper texture as a new layer.
6. Set the texture layer to **Multiply** or **Overlay** mode.

Tips for Using Filters Effectively:

- **Work on Duplicates**: Always duplicate your layer before applying a destructive filter.
- **Use Layer Masks**: Apply filters only to specific areas using masks.
- **Preview First**: Most filters show a preview—take advantage of it!
- **Keep It Subtle**: It's easy to go overboard. Subtle effects often look more professional.
- **Combine with Selections**: You can limit filters to just a selected region for more control.

Chapter 13

Working with Plug-ins and Add-ons

One of the reasons GIMP has gained such popularity is its extensibility. GIMP's open-source nature allows for a rich ecosystem of **plug-ins** and **add-ons** that can extend the software's functionality. Whether you need a specialized tool for photo manipulation, additional filters, or automation scripts, GIMP's plug-in support can make your workflow more efficient and open up creative possibilities.

Finding and Installing Plug-ins

Plug-ins are extensions that add new features or tools to GIMP. You can download them from a variety of websites, and many are freely available due to GIMP's open-source nature.

Where to Find Plug-ins:

1. **Official GIMP Plug-ins Registry:**

- GIMP has an official plug-ins site where you can browse and download many useful plug-ins.
- Visit the GIMP Plugin Registry for a wide variety of tools and effects.

2. **Third-Party Sites and Communities:**

- Sites like **GitHub** and **GIMPChat** often host plug-ins and scripts. Many plug-ins are shared on forums or personal websites by developers.
- Be cautious when downloading from unofficial sources. Ensure you're downloading from trusted sites to avoid potential security risks.

3. **GIMP's Built-In Plug-in Manager:**

- GIMP comes with a built-in plug-in manager where you can browse and enable/disable installed plug-ins.
- This is found under **Edit > Preferences > Folders > Plug-ins**. Here, you can manage locations where GIMP searches for plug-ins.

Installing Plug-ins:

Once you've found the plug-in you want, the installation process is usually straightforward:

1. **Download the Plug-in:**

   - Most plug-ins come as compressed .zip files or .tar.gz archives.
   - Extract the contents if necessary.

2. **Install the Plug-in:**

   - For most systems, you simply place the downloaded plug-in file in the appropriate directory:
   - After copying the plug-in file, restart GIMP.

3. **Check in GIMP:**

   - Open GIMP and check if the new plug-in appears in the **Filters** menu or its appropriate location. Some plug-ins may have custom menus or dialogs.

Troubleshooting:

   - If a plug-in isn't appearing, make sure it's in the correct folder. Also, verify whether the plug-in is compatible with your GIMP version.

- Check for missing dependencies or additional instructions in the plug-in's documentation.

Popular GIMP Plug-ins

There are thousands of GIMP plug-ins, but some have become favorites due to their versatility, ease of use, and added functionality. Let's explore a few popular ones:

1. G'MIC (GREYC's Magic for Image Computing)

G'MIC is one of the most powerful plug-ins available for GIMP. It's a comprehensive framework for image processing, containing over **500 filters** ranging from color adjustments and noise reduction to artistic effects and texture generation.

Key Features:

- Advanced artistic effects (e.g., oil painting, sketching).
- Specialized tools for repairing and enhancing images.

- Customizable filters for unique results.

How to Install:

- Download G'MIC from here.
- Follow the installation instructions based on your operating system.

Once installed, you'll find it under **Filters > G'MIC-Qt**.

2. Resynthesizer

Resynthesizer is a **content-aware fill** plug-in, making it similar to Photoshop's **Content-Aware Fill**. It's particularly useful for removing unwanted objects from images and filling in the gaps seamlessly.

Key Features:

- Remove unwanted elements from photos (e.g., people, logos).
- Fill selected areas with a content-aware algorithm.
- Comes with an option for **texture generation** to create custom backgrounds.

How to Install:

- Download from the Resynthesizer website.
- Follow installation instructions for your system.

3. Layer Effects

Layer Effects is a plug-in that adds Photoshop-style layer styles (like shadows, glows, and embossing) to GIMP.

Key Features:

- Apply styles such as **drop shadows**, **outer glows**, **inner glows**, and **bevels**.
- Quickly tweak layer styles via the Layer Effects dialog.

How to Install:

- Download from the GIMP Plugin Registry.
- Copy the plugin to the **plug-ins** folder and restart GIMP.

4. BIMP (Batch Image Manipulation Plugin)

BIMP is a batch-processing plug-in that allows you to apply multiple edits to a set of images automatically. It's perfect for resizing, cropping, and renaming large numbers of files at once.

Key Features:

- Apply operations to entire directories of images.
- Supports resizing, renaming, format conversion, and more.
- Option to save output in different formats.

How to Install:

- Download from the BIMP website.
- Follow installation instructions for your platform.

Script-Fu and Python-Fu Basics

Beyond installing plug-ins, you can create your own custom tools using scripting. GIMP supports two major scripting languages: **Script-Fu** (based on Scheme) and **Python-Fu** (Python scripting).

Script-Fu:

Script-Fu is GIMP's built-in scripting language based on **Scheme**. It allows users to automate repetitive tasks and create custom functions.

Python-Fu:

Python-Fu allows for much more flexibility and power, especially for users familiar with Python. You can write advanced scripts for tasks like manipulating layers, interacting with external APIs, and handling complex image processing tasks.

GIMP's plug-in and scripting capabilities significantly enhance its functionality, allowing you to automate tasks, extend its feature set, and customize your workflow. Whether you're using ready-made plug-ins like G'MIC or developing your own scripts in Python or Script-Fu, the possibilities for creativity and efficiency are vast.

Chapter 14

Creating Transparent Backgrounds

Transparent backgrounds are essential for a wide range of design and photo-editing projects. Whether you're creating logos, exporting cutouts for video overlays, or isolating objects for graphic design, mastering transparency in GIMP is a must.

Alpha Channels Explained

Transparency in GIMP is controlled through **alpha channels**. Just as an image has channels for red, green, and blue, it can also include an **alpha channel**—a fourth channel that defines the transparency of each pixel.

- **White in alpha** means full opacity.
- **Black** means complete transparency.
- **Gray** represents partial transparency.

How to Check for an Alpha Channel:

1. Open your image.
2. Go to **Layer > Transparency**.
3. If "Add Alpha Channel" is **grayed out**, your image already has one.
4. If it's clickable, select it to add an alpha channel.

Once an alpha channel is present, you can erase parts of the image to transparency instead of a solid background color.

Isolating Subjects

Removing the background to isolate a subject is one of the most common editing tasks in GIMP. The method you use depends on the image's complexity. Let's explore a few techniques:

1. Using the Fuzzy Select Tool (Magic Wand)

Ideal for high-contrast backgrounds or when the subject has clearly defined edges.

Steps:

- Select the **Fuzzy Select Tool** from the toolbox or press **U**.

- Click on the background. Adjust **threshold** to select more or less of the similar color.
- Press **Delete** to remove the background (make sure alpha channel is added).
- Repeat as needed.

Tip: If the background is complex, this tool may leave jagged edges. Use the **Feather** option before deleting to soften the selection edge.

2. Using the Select by Color Tool

Best for uniform color backgrounds (like green screens).

Steps:

- Choose **Select > By Color** from the menu or press **Shift + O**.
- Click the color you want to remove.
- Press **Delete** to make it transparent.

You can also **invert the selection** (Select > Invert) to keep the subject instead of deleting it.

3. Using the Paths Tool (for Precision)

Best for images where subjects are complex or have fine details like hair or intricate shapes.

Steps:

- Select the **Paths Tool (B)** from the toolbox.
- Click to place anchor points around the subject. Curve the lines by clicking and dragging.
- Once the path is complete, press **Enter** to turn it into a selection.
- Invert the selection (**Select > Invert**) and delete the background.

Tip: This method is time-consuming but offers **maximum control** and clean edges.

4. Using Layer Masks

Layer masks are great for **non-destructive editing**. Instead of permanently deleting the background, you simply hide it.

Steps:

- Add a **layer mask** to your image (**Layer > Mask > Add Layer Mask**).
- Choose **White (full opacity)**.
- Use a black brush to paint over the background—it will become transparent.
- Use gray to create soft transitions.
- White brings the masked parts back.

Bonus: This method allows you to fine-tune your selection anytime.

5. Quick Mask Mode

For intricate selections, the **Quick Mask** is ideal.

Steps:

- Click the **Quick Mask button** at the bottom-left of the image window (or press **Shift + Q**).
- Paint over the subject with **black** to mask it, white to unmask.
- Press **Shift + Q** again to return to selection mode.
- Delete or mask the background as needed.

This gives you **brush-level control** over selections.

Saving as PNG with Transparency

Once your subject is isolated and the background is removed or masked, it's time to export your image with a transparent background. The **PNG** format is ideal because it supports full alpha transparency.

Steps to Export with Transparency:

1. Go to **File > Export As**.
2. Choose **.png** as the file extension (e.g., logo.png).
3. Click **Export**.
4. In the pop-up dialog, ensure that the **"Save color values from transparent pixels"** and **"Save background color"** options are unchecked (unless you need them).
5. Click **Export** again.

Common Mistakes to Avoid

1. **Forgetting to Add an Alpha Channel:** If you try to delete the background without one, it will turn white or the background color instead of transparent.

2. **Not Exporting as PNG:** JPEG and BMP formats **do not support transparency**. Make sure you select **PNG** or **GIF** for transparent images (PNG is preferred for quality).
3. **Leaving Edge Halos:** If you delete the background but see a white or colored glow around your subject, try feathering the edge or using **Layer > Transparency > Alpha to Selection** to clean it up.
4. **Using the Eraser Without an Alpha Channel:** The eraser will reveal the background color unless an alpha channel exists.

Bonus Tip: Adding Drop Shadows to Transparent Subjects

To add dimension to your transparent image:

- Duplicate the isolated subject layer.
- Move the bottom layer slightly.
- Fill it with black and blur it (**Filters > Blur > Gaussian Blur**).
- Lower the opacity to create a soft **drop shadow**.

Creating transparent backgrounds is an essential skill in image editing and design. With GIMP's robust toolset—from selection tools and layer masks to advanced export options—you can isolate and save your subjects cleanly and professionally. Whether you're prepping assets for websites, logos for branding, or elements for video, knowing how to use alpha channels and transparency will elevate your workflow.

Chapter 15

Batch Editing and Automation

In digital image editing, efficiency is key—especially when working with dozens or hundreds of images. Repeating the same steps over and over again can be time-consuming, tedious, and prone to error. Thankfully, GIMP offers tools and plug-ins that enable **batch editing** and **automation**, making it easy to apply consistent edits across multiple files in one go.

In this chapter, you'll learn how to use the **BIMP (Batch Image Manipulation Plug-in)**, how to **automate common tasks**, and how to **export multiple files at once**—saving you hours of repetitive work.

Using BIMP (Batch Image Manipulation Plug-in)

The **Batch Image Manipulation Plug-in**, commonly known as **BIMP**, is a must-have tool for anyone who wants to process multiple images simultaneously. It allows you to apply a series of predefined edits—like resizing, renaming, cropping, or format conversion—to entire folders of images with just a few clicks.

Installing BIMP:

1. **Download BIMP** from the official website
2. Choose the correct version for your operating system (Windows, macOS, or Linux).
3. Follow the installation instructions.
4. Once installed, you can launch it from **File > Batch Image Manipulation...**

How BIMP Works:

When you open BIMP, a dialog box appears with several key sections:

- **Add Images or Folders:** Choose individual images or entire directories for processing.
- **Set of Manipulations:** This is where you define what actions BIMP should perform.
- **Output Settings:** Specify the filename pattern, file format, and output folder.

- **Resize:** Scale all selected images to specific dimensions or by a percentage.
- **Crop:** Trim the edges based on fixed values or aspect ratios.
- **Flip/Rotate:** Rotate or flip all images uniformly.
- **Color Correction:** Adjust brightness, contrast, saturation, or apply automatic color levels.
- **Watermarking:** Overlay a logo or text on every image.
- **Format Conversion:** Convert all images to another file format, such as PNG or JPEG.
- **Rename in Bulk:** Set up custom naming patterns to organize your output files.

Once everything is configured, click **Apply** and BIMP will process all the images in the background, freeing you up to focus on more creative tasks.

Automating Common Tasks

Beyond BIMP, GIMP offers other tools and scripting options to automate your workflow. This includes using built-in commands, custom macros, or full scripting languages like **Script-Fu** or **Python-Fu**.

1. Using Image Templates

If you frequently create the same kind of image (e.g., a social media post layout), you can save a **GIMP template** with guides, layers, and elements already in place.

How to Create a Template:

- Set up your layout.
- Save it as an .XCF file (GIMP's native format).
- Reuse it by opening and saving a copy with new content.

2. Saving Tool Presets

You can also save custom tool presets—for brushes, colors, or transformations—using the **Tool Options** dialog.

- Make your adjustments.
- Click the small icon in the Tool Options panel (usually a gear icon).
- Choose **Save Tool Preset** and give it a name.

This is useful for speeding up repetitive tasks with consistent settings.

3. Creating Scripts for Automation

If you're comfortable with scripting, GIMP allows you to write your own automation scripts using either **Script-Fu** (Scheme-based) or **Python-Fu**.

Exporting Multiple Files at Once

Once you've batch-edited your images, exporting them quickly is just as important. GIMP doesn't have a built-in bulk export feature, but you can use plug-ins or scripts to make the process easier.

1. Using BIMP to Export Files

BIMP's final step allows you to export all processed files with:

- A specified **naming convention**.
- A custom **file format** (e.g., convert everything to .png).
- Controlled **quality settings** for compressed formats like JPEG.

2. Export Layers as Files Plug-in

This plug-in allows you to **export every visible layer** in your image as a separate file—perfect for animation frames, sprite sheets, or layered designs.

Steps:

1. Download and install the plug-in (search "export layers GIMP plug-in").
2. Once installed, go to **File > Export Layers**.
3. Configure the output location, file type, and naming pattern.

Whether you're resizing dozens of photos, renaming them, converting file formats, or applying edits like brightness correction and watermarking, GIMP offers robust tools to help you automate these repetitive tasks. Tools like **BIMP**, along with scripting in **Python-Fu** or **Script-Fu**, put you in full control of batch editing workflows.

Chapter 16

Design Projects for Beginners

GIMP isn't just a photo editing tool—it's a powerful graphic design platform capable of helping beginners create stunning visuals. Whether you're designing a catchy social media post, a professional-looking flyer, or a clean logo, GIMP has all the essential tools to bring your creative ideas to life.

Creating Social Media Graphics

Social media platforms like Instagram, Facebook, and Twitter rely heavily on eye-catching visuals. Designing a post that grabs attention and communicates your message clearly is a crucial skill for content creators and marketers.

Step-by-Step Guide:

1. Set Up the Canvas:

- Go to **File > New**.
- Choose dimensions based on platform:

- Instagram: **1080 x 1080 px**
- Facebook post: **1200 x 630 px**
- Twitter: **1600 x 900 px**
- Set the resolution to **72 PPI** for screen-based content.

2. Add a Background:

- Use the **Bucket Fill Tool** or **Gradient Tool** to create a background.
- Consider using soft gradients, textures, or a high-resolution image as the base.

3. Insert Your Image or Graphic:

- Drag and drop your image into the canvas or go to **File > Open as Layers**.
- Scale it using **Shift + S** or the **Scale Tool** to fit your layout.

4. Add Text:

- Use the **Text Tool (T)** to add a headline or caption.
- Choose bold, readable fonts.
- Consider using font pairs (a bold font for titles, a clean font for supporting text).

5. Apply Effects:

- Add a **drop shadow**: Right-click the text layer > **Alpha to Selection** > Create a new layer > Fill with black > Blur using **Gaussian Blur**.
- Adjust color balance, brightness, or saturation to make the design pop.

6. Export for Web:

- Go to **File > Export As**.

Tips:

- Keep your design clean and focused.
- Use contrast to make text stand out.
- Stick to a color scheme that matches your brand or theme.

Making a Poster or Flyer

Posters and flyers are excellent tools for promoting events, products, or causes. GIMP gives you the flexibility to design high-resolution prints that are both professional and creative.

Step-by-Step Guide:

1. Set the Canvas Size:

- Go to **File > New**.
- Use standard print dimensions:
- A4: **210 x 297 mm (2480 x 3508 px at 300 DPI)**
- US Letter: **8.5 x 11 inches (2550 x 3300 px at 300 DPI)**
- Set **Resolution to 300 PPI** for print quality.

2. Layout the Design:

- Add **guides** for margins: **Image > Guides > New Guide (by Percent)** or manually drag from rulers.
- Use **Grids (View > Show Grid)** for alignment.

3. Add Background and Visual Elements:

- Use high-resolution images or gradients.
- Import logos, shapes, and branding elements with **File > Open as Layers**.

4. Add Text Blocks:

- Headline: Clear, bold text at the top.
- Subheading: Smaller font with supporting info.
- Body: Event details, contact info, etc.

5. Highlight Key Info:

- Use contrasting colors or boxes to emphasize dates, prices, or calls-to-action.

6. Use Layer Groups:

- Group related layers (e.g., all text or all graphics) for easy editing.

7. Export for Print:

- Save as **.XCF** for future edits.
- Export as **PDF** or **PNG/JPEG at 300 DPI** for printing.

Tips:

- Maintain visual hierarchy (biggest elements = most important).
- Don't overcrowd—use whitespace strategically.
- Choose high-quality fonts and images.

Designing a Simple Logo

Logos are fundamental to branding. With GIMP, you can design a clean, scalable logo that represents a business, project, or personal brand.

Step-by-Step Guide:

1. Set Up a Transparent Canvas:

- Go to **File > New**.
- Use a square size like **1000 x 1000 px**.
- Under "Advanced Options," select **Fill with: Transparency**.
- Add an **Alpha Channel** if not present.

2. Sketch or Plan Your Concept:

- Before jumping into the design, think about:

a. What does the logo represent?
b. Should it be text-only, icon-based, or a mix?

3. Create Shapes and Icons:

- Use the **Ellipse, Rectangle, or Path Tool** to form your base shapes.

- Apply strokes and fills with the **Bucket Fill** or **Stroke Path** options.
- Keep the design simple and bold.

4. Add Text:

- Use the **Text Tool** for your brand name.
- Experiment with **kerning** (spacing between letters) for custom feel.
- Use custom fonts if necessary (install TTF fonts on your OS, then restart GIMP).

5. Combine Elements:

- Align everything using **Guides** and **Align Tool**.
- Merge layers only when you're sure about placement.

6. Export with Transparency:

- Export as **.PNG** with transparent background.
- Use high resolution (300 DPI) and scale down as needed later.

Tips:

- Stick to 2-3 colors max.

- Avoid detailed designs: Simplicity equals versatility.
- Test how your logo looks small and large.

These beginner design projects give you practical experience with GIMP's powerful tools while building essential design skills. From creating attention-grabbing social media posts to crafting professional flyers and building brand identity through logos, these projects help bridge the gap between theory and real-world application.

Chapter 17

Photo Manipulation Projects

Photo manipulation is where creativity truly meets technical skill. With GIMP's extensive toolset, you can transform ordinary images into something extraordinary—whether it's replacing a dull background, combining different elements from multiple images, or creating surreal, dreamlike compositions. In this chapter, we'll walk through three hands-on photo manipulation projects to help you build your confidence and skill set: **replacing backgrounds**, **combining multiple images**, and **creating surreal compositions**.

Replacing Backgrounds

Removing or replacing the background of an image is one of the most commonly used photo manipulation techniques. It can make your subject stand out, clean up a messy background, or transport your subject into a new scene altogether.

Step-by-Step Guide:

1. Open Your Subject Image:

- Load the image you want to manipulate using **File > Open**.

2. Isolate the Subject:

- Use the **Free Select Tool**, **Paths Tool**, or **Foreground Select Tool** to create a selection around your subject.
- Once selected, go to **Select > Invert**, then press **Delete** to remove the background (ensure there's an Alpha Channel added via **Layer > Transparency > Add Alpha Channel**).

3. Clean the Edges:

- Zoom in and use **Feathering** or **Refine Edge** to smooth out harsh lines.
- Use the **Eraser Tool** with a soft brush to manually touch up tricky spots like hair or fur.

4. Add the New Background:

- Open the background image in GIMP.

- Copy and paste it as a new layer **below** the subject.
- Scale or move the background as needed using the **Scale Tool** and **Move Tool**.

5. Match Lighting and Color:

- Use **Color Balance**, **Brightness/Contrast**, or **Hue/Saturation** on the subject to match the background's tone.
- Optionally, add a shadow beneath the subject using a **blurred black shape** with reduced opacity.

Tips:

- Use **layer masks** to non-destructively hide background parts.
- For hair or complex edges, try **Quick Mask Mode** and refine with a soft brush.

Combining Multiple Images

Combining multiple images—often called compositing—lets you create stunning new scenes. This technique is great for collages, digital art, or promotional content.

Step-by-Step Guide:

1. Choose Compatible Images:

- Pick photos that share similar **lighting**, **angle**, and **resolution** for a more natural blend.
- Download from free stock photo sites or use your own photography.

2. Open All Images as Layers:

- Use **File > Open as Layers** to stack all the images into one project file.

3. Arrange and Resize:

- Use the **Move Tool** to position each image.
- Use the **Scale Tool** to resize them so they blend naturally.

4. Use Masks for Blending:

- Apply a **layer mask** to each image.
- Paint with black on the mask to hide parts, and white to reveal.
- Use a **soft brush** with low opacity for seamless transitions.

5. Match Colors and Light:

- Adjust each image using **Colors > Levels, Curves**, or **Color Balance.**
- Add shadows and highlights for realism— soft black or white shapes with **Gaussian Blur** work well.

6. Add Finishing Touches:

- Add overlays like light leaks, lens flares, or textures to unify the images.
- Use adjustment layers or duplicate the final composition and apply a global color grade.

Tips:

- Pay attention to perspective. Use guides or vanishing points to keep objects aligned.
- Use filters like **Blur > Gaussian Blur** to match depth of field across different images.

Creating Surreal Compositions

Surreal compositions allow you to bend reality and dive into fantasy. These projects are a great way to experiment creatively and practice combining multiple techniques.

Creative Ideas to Try:

- A person floating in the sky surrounded by clouds.
- A tree growing from the top of a head.
- A fish swimming through a forest.

Step-by-Step Guide:

1. Concept First:

- Start with a simple sketch or idea. Surrealism works best when there's a core concept or emotion behind it.

2. Collect Your Assets:

- Choose images that support your theme. Look for high-resolution photos of people, landscapes, animals, or objects.

3. Build the Base Scene:

- Open a background image to serve as the "stage."
- Add objects or people using **Open as Layers**, then isolate them using **layer masks** or **selection tools**.

4. Experiment with Scale and Position:

- Make small objects huge, or large objects tiny.
- Flip or rotate layers to create unexpected effects.

5. Add Surreal Effects:

- Use **smoke brushes**, **nebula overlays**, or **distortion filters** to add dreamlike elements.
- Try **Layer Modes** like Overlay, Soft Light, or Multiply to blend textures or effects.

6. Use the Path Tool for Details:

- Create floating ribbons, swirling paths, or unnatural shapes using the **Path Tool**, then **Stroke Path** with custom brushes.

7. Color Grade for Unity:

- Use **Color Look-Up Tables (CLUTs)** or manual grading (Levels, Curves) to unify the colors and lighting.
- Try adding a vignette to focus the viewer's attention.

8. Final Polish:

- Zoom in and clean up edges.
- Add shadows or light to boost realism.
- Use **Filters > Light and Shadow > Drop Shadow** or **Perspective Shadow** for dramatic effects.

Tips:

- **Less is more:** Avoid overcrowding your scene.
- Use light and shadow to create focus and mood.
- **Take your time with details:** They make all the difference.

Photo manipulation projects not only allow you to express your creativity but also give you real experience using GIMP's most powerful features—from selections and masks to blending and effects. Whether you're replacing a background for a professional headshot, merging scenes for an advertisement, or diving deep into surreal visual storytelling, the skills you develop here will open doors to limitless visual possibilities.

As always, practice is key. Don't be afraid to experiment with layers, tools, and techniques to discover your unique style and workflow. The more you explore, the more confident and skilled you'll become.

Chapter 18

Tips for Seniors and Accessibility

GIMP is a powerful tool for image editing and design, but like many advanced software applications, it can feel overwhelming—especially for seniors or users who prefer a simplified, accessible workspace. Fortunately, GIMP 3 includes several features and customizations that make it easier to use for individuals with varying needs, including visual, motor, and cognitive considerations.

This chapter is dedicated to **making GIMP more user-friendly and ergonomic** for seniors and anyone seeking a more accessible editing environment. Whether you're a retiree learning digital art, someone managing limited mobility, or simply looking for a more comfortable workspace, these tips will help you tailor GIMP to your preferences.

Simplifying the Interface

A cluttered or overly complex interface can hinder creativity and productivity. GIMP's customizable layout allows users to streamline their workspace by hiding unnecessary tools and panels.

1. Activate Single-Window Mode:

- Go to **Windows > Single-Window Mode**.
- This removes the floating windows and arranges everything into one main window—much easier to manage.

2. Close Unnecessary Panels:

GIMP shows many toolboxes and docks by default. You can simplify the view by closing any you don't need:

- Right-click on any tab (like "Tool Options" or "Layers").
- Select **Close Tab** to remove it.

Only keep essentials, like:

- Tool Options
- Layers
- Brushes or Fonts

3. Save a Custom Workspace:

Once you've cleaned up the interface, save it for future use:

- Go to **Edit > Preferences > Window Management.**
- Click **Save Window Positions Now.**

4. Customize the Toolbox:

- Go to **Edit > Preferences > Toolbox.**
- You can choose which tools are shown. For example, if you don't use paths or color pickers, you can uncheck them.

5. Increase Icon Visibility:

- Under **Edit > Preferences > Icon Theme,** choose a theme with larger, high-contrast icons for better visibility.

Tip: The "Color" theme with the "Symbolic" icon set is especially clean and easy on the eyes.

Using Larger Fonts and Icons

Visual clarity is essential—especially for users with reduced vision. GIMP allows you to adjust font sizes, icon sizes, and color schemes for better readability and usability.

1. Change the Interface Font Size:

- Go to **Edit > Preferences > Interface > Font**.
- Increase the font size to your comfort level (14–18pt is often ideal for seniors).
- You may need to restart GIMP for changes to fully apply.

2. Adjust Icon Size:

- Go to **Edit > Preferences > Icon Theme**.
- Choose an icon size from:
- Small
- Medium
- Large
- Huge (best for high-resolution monitors or low vision).

3. Use High-Contrast Themes:

- Under **Edit > Preferences > Theme**, select a theme with strong contrast.
- "System" or "Dark" themes often work well depending on your lighting environment.

- "Light" theme with dark text may be preferable for those with certain vision conditions.

4. Zoom In on Canvases:

- Use the + **(plus key)** or **Ctrl + Mouse Wheel Up** to zoom in on your project for easier editing.
- GIMP supports zooming up to 3200%, which helps when working on tiny details or correcting small areas.

Tip: Consider changing the **canvas background** to a neutral color to reduce eye strain. Right-click the canvas area > **Configure Canvas Background**.

Ergonomic Editing Techniques

Comfort and ease of use are vital when working for extended periods—especially for older users. Here are tips to make your editing sessions more ergonomic and less physically demanding.

1. Use Keyboard Shortcuts Wisely:

- Memorize just a few shortcuts to avoid excess mouse movement:

- **Ctrl + Z**: Undo
- **Ctrl + S**: Save
- **Ctrl + Shift + E**: Export
- **B**: Brush Tool
- **T**: Text Tool
- You can even **customize your own shortcuts** under **Edit > Keyboard Shortcuts**.

2. Use a Comfortable Mouse or Stylus:

- A wireless ergonomic mouse or pen tablet (like Wacom) can reduce wrist strain.
- Styluses offer more natural movement, especially useful for painting or retouching.

3. Limit Drag-and-Drop Tasks:

- Instead of dragging layers or selections, use the **Move Tool** with arrow keys for more precision and less strain.

4. Break Projects into Sessions:

- Long editing sessions can be tiring. Save your work regularly and take short breaks every 20–30 minutes.
- Use **File > Save As** to create iterative versions, just in case.

5. Use Guides and Align Tools:

- Aligning items manually can be tough. Use **Image > Guides > New Guide (by Percent)** to help center elements.
- Or use the **Align Tool** (Q) to auto-align layers and objects.

6. Enable Tooltips and Help:

- If you forget what a button does, hover your cursor over it—GIMP provides **tooltip descriptions.**
- Access the **Help System** with **F1**, or visit **Help > User Manual** for detailed guidance.

The best workspace is the one that feels intuitive, comfortable, and free from distractions. By simplifying GIMP's interface, increasing font and icon sizes, and using ergonomic tools and shortcuts, seniors and accessibility-conscious users can enjoy the full potential of this powerful program without feeling overwhelmed or fatigued.

Chapter 19

Troubleshooting Common Issues

Even with a robust program like GIMP 3, you may occasionally encounter issues that disrupt your workflow—whether it's a tool behaving unexpectedly, performance lag, or trouble saving your project. This chapter provides solutions to some of the most common issues GIMP users face, with practical tips to help you fix, prevent, and recover from problems quickly and efficiently.

Fixing Tool Problems

Sometimes a tool doesn't respond the way you expect, or it seems like it isn't working at all. Before assuming something is broken, there are a few quick checks and fixes you can try.

1. Tool Not Working Properly? Check These First:

- **Check the Active Layer:** Make sure you're working on the correct layer. If a layer is invisible, locked, or empty, the tool won't behave as expected. Check layer visibility (the eye icon) and layer opacity.
- **Verify Tool Options:** Every tool has its own settings in the **Tool Options** dock. For example, if the **Brush Tool** seems weak, check the opacity and hardness settings. They may be set too low.
- **Reset Tool to Default:** Right-click on the tool's icon in the toolbox and select Reset Tool Options. Alternatively, go to Edit > Preferences > Tool Options, and click Reset Saved Tool Options to Default Values.
- **Make Sure No Selection Is Active:** If you accidentally made a selection and it's still active, your tool will only affect the selected area. Press **Ctrl + Shift + A** to deselect everything.
- **Check the Paint Mode:** Many paint tools have blending modes (e.g., Multiply, Overlay). If a non-standard mode is selected, it might make your tool look like

it's not working. Set the mode to **Normal** for standard use.

2. Common Tool-Specific Issues:

- **Move Tool Won't Move the Layer:** In the **Tool Options**, make sure it's set to **Move the Active Layer**, not just the selection or path.
- **Text Tool Won't Show Changes:** Check if you're editing an existing text layer. If the font or size isn't updating, deselect the text and try again after clicking outside the text box.
- **Selection Tools Behaving Strangely:** Look at the **mode** (Replace, Add, Subtract, Intersect) in the **Tool Options**. Sometimes the wrong mode causes confusing results.

Performance Tweaks

GIMP is lightweight compared to many commercial editors, but on older systems or with high-resolution images, performance can become sluggish. Here's how to speed things up.

1. Adjust Tile Cache Size:

- Go to **Edit** > **Preferences** > **System Resources**.
- Increase the **Tile Cache Size** to allow GIMP to use more RAM for processing images.
- For example, increase it from 512 MB to 2048 MB if you have 8 GB or more of system RAM.

2. Limit Undo Levels:

- GIMP stores many undo steps, which can consume memory.
- In **Preferences** > **System Resources**, reduce the **Undo Levels** to around 10–20 for better performance.

3. Use Smaller Image Sizes When Possible:

- Extremely large images (like 10,000 x 10,000 pixels) use a lot of resources.
- For web graphics or practice projects, scale down your canvas to something manageable.

4. Disable Real-Time Previews:

- Some tools (like **Filters** or **Color Adjustments**) show real-time previews that can slow down GIMP.
- If your system is lagging, disable previews in those dialog boxes before applying changes.

5. Close Unused Dock Panels and Layers:

- More visible panels and layers = more memory usage.
- Hide or delete anything you don't need during editing.

6. Keep GIMP and Plug-ins Updated:

- Updates often fix bugs and improve performance.

Saving and Recovery Options

Lost work or corrupted files can be a nightmare—but GIMP offers several features to help you save regularly and recover lost projects.

1. Best Saving Practices:

- **Use the Native Format (.XCF):** Always save your working files in **.XCF** to preserve layers, masks, paths, and guides. Use **File > Save** or **Ctrl + S** frequently during a project.
- **Use Descriptive File Names and Versions:** Add version numbers or dates to your files to avoid overwriting earlier stages.
- **Export for Final Output:** Use **File > Export As** to save in JPG, PNG, or other formats. Choose PNG for high-quality, lossless output and transparency support.

2. Auto-Save with Plug-ins:

- GIMP doesn't have built-in auto-save, but some plug-ins (like **Resynthesizer** or third-party auto-save tools) offer that functionality.
- You can also set reminders or use OS-level backup solutions like **File History (Windows)** or **Time Machine (Mac)**.

3. Recovering Unsaved Work:

- If GIMP crashes, it may offer to **recover files** when you reopen the application.

- If prompted, choose **Recover** and save immediately under a new name.
- Check your system's **temp folders** if no recovery option appears:
- Some Linux distros allow background session autosaves via session management tools.

4. File Won't Open or Save? Try This:

- **Unsupported File Type:** Make sure the format is supported (.jpg, .png, .tiff, .bmp, .gif, .xcf, etc.). Some RAW files from cameras may require a plug-in like **Darktable** or **RawTherapee**.
- **Corrupted File:** Try opening the file in another app to confirm the issue. Open a copy of the file in GIMP, then try exporting it to a different format.
- **Permission Issues:** Make sure the folder you're saving to is writable. On some systems, running GIMP as administrator may help.

Troubleshooting doesn't have to be intimidating. By learning a few diagnostic steps—like checking your tool settings, adjusting performance preferences, and practicing smart saving habits—you'll be able to fix most common issues on your own and avoid losing your hard work.

Chapter 20

Advancing Your Skills and Next Steps

Congratulations! If you've made it this far, you've journeyed through the core features of GIMP 3 and explored tools, techniques, and workflows to elevate your image editing and graphic design capabilities. But like any creative craft, mastering GIMP is a continuous process. This final chapter is your guide to what comes next—where to deepen your knowledge, how to stay inspired, and how GIMP stacks up against the industry giant, Photoshop.

Where to Learn More

GIMP has a dedicated global community and plenty of free (and paid) resources for continued learning. Here are a few trusted ways to expand your skills beyond this guide:

1. GIMP's Official Documentation and Tutorials

- Visit the official GIMP documentation at https://docs.gimp.org for the most detailed and up-to-date instructions.
- The site includes tutorials on basic and advanced features, from selections to scripting.

2. YouTube Channels

- Visual learning is often more effective, especially for creative software. Popular YouTube channels that regularly post GIMP tutorials:
- Davies Media Design
- Logos by Nick
- Chris' Tutorials
- PhotoAdvanced

Whether you're interested in digital painting, photo retouching, or graphic design, you'll find playlists tailored to your goals.

3. Online Courses

- Platforms like **Udemy**, **Skillshare**, and **Coursera** offer structured GIMP courses—great if you prefer a curriculum-like experience.

- These courses are often taught by professionals and include downloadable resources, assignments, and community interaction.

4. eBooks and PDFs

- Many GIMP power users have created detailed PDF guides and books available online or in print. Search Amazon or other eBook platforms for terms like:
- *"Advanced GIMP Techniques"*
- *"Digital Painting with GIMP"*

Joining the GIMP Community

One of GIMP's greatest strengths is its active, helpful community. Participating in user forums, open-source groups, or design contests can help you stay motivated and up-to-date with new features or plug-ins.

1. Online Forums and Subreddits

- **GIMP Chat:** One of the longest-running GIMP user forums.

- **Reddit (/r/GIMP)**: A thriving community for Q&A, critiques, and project showcases.
- **DeviantArt (GIMP users group)**: A great place to post your artwork and receive feedback.

2. GIMP Plug-in Registry

- Many users develop and share custom plug-ins for effects, automation, and new tools.
- Websites like **GIMP Plugin Registry** or GitHub repositories provide these resources. Always double-check for compatibility with GIMP 3 before installing.

3. Open-Source Contribution

- If you're tech-savvy or learning to code, you can contribute to GIMP's development.
- GIMP is built on open-source principles, so your help—whether in bug testing, scripting, or documentation—is always welcome.

4. Creative Challenges

- Join monthly challenges hosted by forums or YouTube creators.
- These may include tasks like: *"Design a fantasy creature"* or *"Recreate a famous painting in your own style."*
- They're perfect for building a portfolio while pushing your limits.

Pros of GIMP:

- 100% free, no hidden fees
- Works on all major operating systems
- Fast and lightweight, even on modest hardware
- Deep customization with open-source plug-ins
- A great community for support

Limitations:

- No native CMYK support (important for print)
- Some tools (like smart object editing or advanced typography) are more refined in Photoshop
- UI and workflow may feel different if you've used Adobe tools before

Bottom Line:

GIMP is more than capable for the majority of graphic design and photo editing tasks— especially for beginners, hobbyists, students, and even professionals who prefer open-source software. While Photoshop may be the industry gold standard, GIMP levels the playing field by giving users a free, powerful platform with no strings attached.

If your needs are advanced (like heavy video editing, 3D modeling, or commercial printing), Photoshop might be worth exploring. But if you're comfortable with GIMP—and especially if you supplement it with tools like **Inkscape** (for vector art) or **Krita** (for digital painting)—you can produce studio-quality work without spending a dime.

GIMP 3 opens the door to an exciting world of creative possibilities. From enhancing family photos to designing logos, painting fantasy landscapes, or creating surreal art, you now have the tools and knowledge to bring your vision to life.

Remember:

- **Mastery comes through practice.** Don't be afraid to experiment.
- **The learning never stops.** Stay curious and keep exploring new techniques.
- **Your unique style matters.** Use the tools to express *your* creativity, not just to replicate others.

www.ingramcontent.com/pod-product-compliance
Lightning Source LLC
LaVergne TN
LVHW051239050326
832903LV00028B/2470